Sheep

Rachael Bell

Heinemann

The author wishes to thank Tom Clifford for giving his time and insight.

First published in Great Britain by Heinemann Library
Halley Court, Jordan Hill, Oxford OX2 8EJ,
a division of Reed Educational and Professional Publishing Ltd.
Heinemann is a registered trademark of Reed Educational & Professional Publishing Limited.

OXFORD MELBOURNE AUCKLAND
JOHANNESBURG BLANTYRE GABORONE
IBADAN PORTSMOUTH NH (USA) CHICAGO

Designed by AMR
Originated by Ambassador Litho Ltd
Printed in Hong Kong/China

05 04 03 02 01
10 9 8 7 6 5 4 3 2 1

ISBN 0 431 10088 8
This title is also available in a hardback library edition (ISBN 0 431 10081 0)

British Library Cataloguing in Publication Data
Bell, Rachael, 1972–
  Sheep. – (Farm animals)
  1.Sheep – Juvenile literature
  I.Title
  636.3

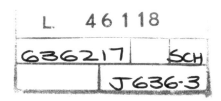

Acknowledgements
The Publishers would like to thank the following for permission to reproduce photographs:
Agripicture p 21/Peter Dean; J Allan Cash Ltd, p 27; Anthony Blake Photo Library p 23/Sue Atkinson; Bruce Coleman pp 8/Jorg & Petra Wegner, 18/Stephen Bond; Farmers Weekly Picture Library pp 11, 13, 19; Holt Studios pp 4 l/Richard Anthony, 12 & 14/Wayne Hutchinson, 15/Primrose Peacock, 24/Gordon Roberts; Chris Honeywell p 25; Images of Nature/FLPA pp 4 r/Tony Hamblin, 5/I. Lee Rue, 6/Derek A. Robinson, 16/Peter Dean, 17/M. J. Thomas, 20/Peter Dean; Martin Sookias, p 22; Lynn M Stone pp 9, 10, 28; Tony Stone Images pp 7/Philip H. Coblentz, 26/Anthony Cassidy, 29/David Woodfall.

Cover photograph reproduced with permission of NHPA.

Our thanks to Tony Prior, Bowers Farm, Wantage, Oxon, for his comments in the preparation of this book.

Every effort has been made to contact copyright holders of any material reproduced in this book. Any omissions will be rectified in subsequent printings if notice is given to the Publisher.

For more information about Heinemann Library books, or to order, please phone 01865 888066, or send a fax to 01865 314091. You can visit our web site at www.heinemann.co.uk

Contents

Sheep relatives   4

Welcome to the sheep farm   6

Meet the sheep   8

Meet the baby sheep   10

Where do sheep live?   12

What do sheep eat?   14

How do sheep stay healthy?   16

How do sheep sleep?   18

Who looks after the sheep?   20

What are sheep kept for?   22

What else are sheep kept for?   24

Other kinds of sheep farm   26

Fact file   28

Glossary   30

More books to read   32

Index   32

Words in bold **like this** are explained in the Glossary.

Sheep relatives

Most sheep are white, but they can also be black or dark brown. Their coats may be long and curly or short and smooth. However they look, they all make a deep 'baa' noise!

Farmers choose sheep that suit where they live, so most sheep in one area look the same. Some sheep live wild, like this Bighorn sheep in North America.

Welcome to the sheep farm

On this farm, the farmer keeps many sheep. He also has a sheep-dog. The sheep-dog is a working animal and is kept outside in the farmyard.

Most of the land on the farm is used for **grazing** the sheep. The rest is used for **crops** like wheat and oats. These are turned into bread or breakfast **cereal**. The **hay** is sold as horse food.

Meet the sheep

tail

udder

The **female** sheep is called a **ewe**.
Ewes have up to three lambs a year.
They take good care of the lambs.
Two lambs can drink milk from their
mother at the same time.

eye   horn

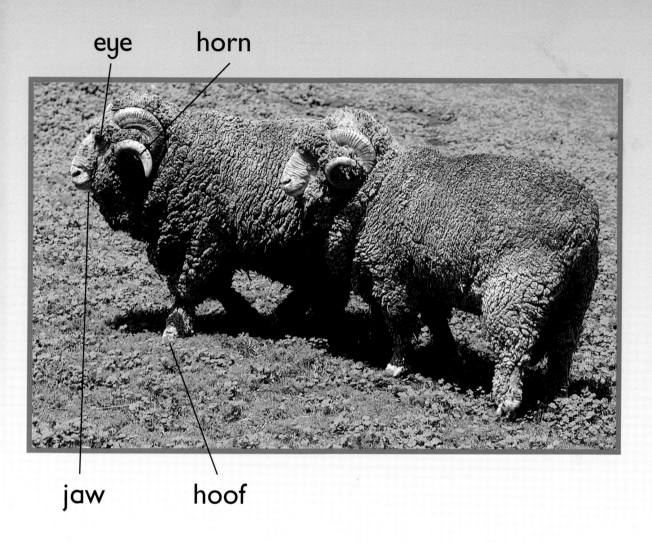

jaw   hoof

The **male** sheep is called a ram. Some rams have horns. They can use them to fight off other rams and **protect** the ewes.

Meet the baby sheep

Baby sheep are called lambs. They can walk within minutes of being born. Lambs make a high-sounding noise, called bleating.

When lambs are very young, they feed on milk from their mother. Before long, the lambs start to eat grass and other food.

Where do sheep live?

Sheep spend most of their life outdoors. They are very tough animals. A sheep's thick **fleece** keeps it warm, even in freezing weather.

At **lambing time**, most sheep are kept in a barn with deep **straw** on the floor. The **ewe** and her lambs go outside again when the lambs are about three weeks old.

What do sheep eat?

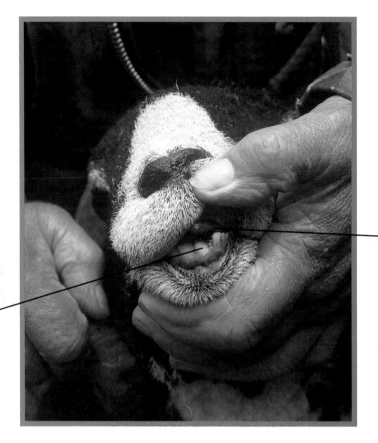

pad in top of mouth

teeth in bottom jaw

Sheep's mouths are made for nibbling short grass. They bite off grass between their bottom front teeth and upper **pad**, then swallow it. Later they **chew the cud** between their back teeth.

In winter when the grass stops growing quickly, sheep eat **hay** and **ewe** nuts. Ewe nuts are made from **cereals**, like your breakfast food. They drink water from **troughs** all year round.

How do sheep stay healthy?

Sheep catch **diseases** and **parasites** very easily. They get them from each other and from the ground. The best way to keep sheep healthy is to make sure they only have fresh grass.

Farmers take good care of their sheep. They dip the sheep in a special liquid to kill any parasites. They also give the sheep **injections** against diseases.

How do sheep sleep?

As it gets dark, the sheep gather together. They find a sheltered area and lie down with their backs to the wind.

Sheep sleep with their eyes closed. If you disturb them, they wake up and run off. Sometimes they **graze** too, but they soon lie down again to rest.

Who looks after the sheep?

The **shepherd** checks the sheep every day in the field with his sheep-dog. The dog runs around the sheep to collect them up and move them to the next field.

The farmer and his shepherd look after the **ewes** when they are inside. Sometimes they trim the sheep's **hooves** – a bit like cutting your nails!

What are sheep kept for?

Most farms keep sheep for their meat. The meat from sheep is called lamb. It can be used in many different dishes.

The main cuts of meat from a lamb
are the shoulder, leg or lamb chop.
This is a roast leg of lamb.

What else are sheep kept for?

Sheep are also kept for their wool. A sheep's **fleece** is **sheared** off – a bit like having a hair cut. The fleece is sent to a factory to be cleaned and spun into wool.

Some farms also keep sheep for their creamy milk. They make special cheeses and yoghurt from it. Roquefort is a famous blue cheese made from **ewes'** milk.

Other kinds of sheep farm

In some parts of the world, farmers keep sheep high up in the mountains. The **shepherd** moves around with his sheep.

In Australia, big sheep farms are called sheep stations. They have many thousands of sheep. The sheep are left alone for most of the year, until they are rounded up for market.

Fact file

 Sheep prefer being together in a **flock**. If one sheep moves, the others follow it.

 Lambs are born with eight **milk teeth**. Every year, two of their milk teeth fall out and are replaced by adult teeth. After only a few years these adult teeth start to fall out.

 When a lamb is about one day old, the farmer puts a tight rubber ring on its tail. This makes the tail fall off. It does not hurt the lamb and stops it getting dirty under the tail.

Sometimes a farmer needs a **ewe** to feed a lamb that is not her own. He holds the lamb where the ewe cannot see or smell it. Soon she gets used to the new lamb and lets it feed from her. If this does not work, the farmer's family feed the lamb from a bottle, just like a baby!

 Sheep's **fleeces** have been used for over 3000 years to make wool. Most families had a spinning wheel to turn the fleece into wool.

Glossary

cereals	wheat, oats and barley, often made into breakfast food
chew the cud	bring food back up into the mouth from the stomach, to chew it again
crops	plants that the farmer grows in his fields
diseases	illnesses
ewe	female or mother sheep
female	the girl or mother
fleece	sheep's coat of wool
flock	group of sheep that live together
graze	eat grass in a field
hay	cut and dried grass
hooves	the hard pads of the sheep's feet
injections	special medicines which are given through a needle
lambing time	when the lambs are born
male	the boy or father
milk teeth	the first teeth
pad	hard area in sheep's mouth

parasites	little animals that live on bigger animals and usually harm them
protect	keep safe
sheared	how the fleece of a sheep is cut off in one bundle
shepherd	man or woman who looks after sheep
straw	thick, dried stalks from crops
trough	food or water container for animals
udder	the sheep's milk bag

More books to read

Story books

I love Animals, Walker Books
Picnic Farm, Macmillan
Over in the Meadow, Walker Books

Information books

Animal Young – Mammals, Heinemann Library
Images – On the Farm, Heinemann Library
The Farming Year, Autumn, Winter, Spring, Summer,
  Wayland
Mealtimes – Evening Meals Around the World, Wayland

Index

Australia 27
ewe 8, 9, 13, 21, 25, 29
cheese 25
fleece 12, 24, 29
food 11, 14, 15
lambs 8, 10, 11, 13, 22,
  28, 29
meat 22, 23

milk 8, 11, 25
mouth 14
ram 9
sheep-dog 6, 20
shepherd 20, 21, 26
sleep 18, 19
teeth 14, 28
wool 24, 29